contents

Key

- Number and Place value
- Addition and Subtraction
- Multiplication and Division
- Shape and Measure
- Fractions
- Mixed Operations

How to use this book

The first page of each section will have a title telling you what the next few pages are about.

Your teacher may tell you to GRAB something that might help you answer the questions.

Read the instructions carefully before each set of questions.

Sometimes a character will give you a tip.

Adding and subtracting by partitioning

GRAB! Base 10 equipment and place-value cards

|35| + |46|

30 + 40 = 70   5 + 6 = 11

70 + 11 = 81

Add these by partitioning.

1. 54 + 37 = ☐
2. 17 + 65 = ☐
3. 28 + 34 = ☐
4. 48 + 36 = ☐
5. 29 + 43 = ☐

6. 33 + 38 = ☐
7. 57 + 26 = ☐
8. 68 + 27 = ☐
9. 16 + 78 = ☐
10. 48 + 35 = ☐

11. 18 + 25 + 34 = ☐

I am confident with adding 2-digit numbers by partitioning.

64

Perform these calculations using partitioning.

1. 35 + 42 = ☐
2. 26 + 31 = ☐
3. 64 + 25 = ☐
4. 33 + 43 = ☐
5. 52 + 37 = ☐
6. 25 + 47 = ☐
7. 36 + 35 = ☐
8. 35 + 48 = ☐
9. 27 + 47 = ☐
10. 45 + 46 = ☐

11. 28 + 66 = ☐
12. 35 + 39 = ☐
13. 55 + 27 = ☐
14. 49 + 42 = ☐
15. 25 + 48 = ☐
16. 38 + 47 = ☐
17. ☐ − 42 = 23
18. ☐ − 35 = 22
19. ☐ − 47 = 36
20. ☐ − 58 = 27

These last ones are not as hard as they look.

Check your answers to questions 17 to 20 using addition.

21. Jade has money in two purses. She has 26p in one and 62p in another. How much has she altogether?

22. Mel's dad weighs 46 kg more than Mel. Mel weighs 28 kg. How much does her dad weigh?

THINK Write as many addition questions as you can using the digits 4, 5, 6 and 7, and answer them.

I am confident with adding 2-digit numbers by partitioning.

65

Some pages will show you an example or model.

Each area of maths has its own colour.

THINK questions will challenge you to think more about the maths on the page.

Choose a traffic light colour to say how confident you are with the maths on the page.

GRAB! A bead string

Complete each addition and subtraction.

1 $65 + \boxed{} = 100$

2 $55 + \boxed{} = 100$

3 $25 + \boxed{} = 100$

4 $100 - \boxed{} = 40$

5 $15 + \boxed{} = 100$

6 $\boxed{} + 70 = 100$

I am confident with multiples of 5 bonds to 100.

Write the missing numbers to complete these bonds to 100.

1. ☐ + 20 = 100

2. 50 + ☐ = 100

3. 100 − ☐ = 30

4. 100 − ☐ = 90

5. ☐ + 60 = 100

6. 0 + ☐ = 100

7. 70 + ☐ = 100

8. 100 − ☐ = 60

9. ☐ + 10 = 100

10. 100 − ☐ = 80

11. Envelopes come in packs of 100. Mrs Lee has used 70 of the envelopes from a pack. How many are left?

12. Kelly has 100 g of crisps. She eats 40 g of them and her brother eats the rest. How much does he eat?

13. Gran puts 40 g of sugar in a bowl. She adds 60 g of flour and mixes. How much does the mix weigh?

14. Stan is driving 100 km. By three o'clock he has driven 80 km. How far has he left to go?

 How many different ways can you split ten 10p coins into two piles? What about three piles?

I am confident with multiples of 10 bonds to 100.

Copy and complete these bonds to 100.

1. $\Box + 65 = 100$

2. $80 + \Box = 100$

3. $100 - \Box = 10$

4. $100 - \Box = 95$

5. $\Box + 45 = 100$

6. $100 - \Box = 35$

7. $100 - \Box = 20$

8. $\Box + 5 = 100$

9. $0 + \Box = 100$

10. $100 - \Box = 15$

11. $55 + \Box = 100$

12. $100 - \Box = 40$

13. $\Box + 85 = 100$

14. $100 - 70 = \Box$

15. $75 + 25 = \Box$

16. $100 - \Box = 30$

17. Seaton school has 100 raffle tickets. It sells 85 of them. How many tickets are there still to sell?

18. On the field is a 100 m track. Jo starts at one end and hops for 25 m. She then runs the rest. How far did she run?

Put twenty 5p coins into two piles. How much money is in each pile? How many different ways can you do this?

I am confident with multiples of 5 bonds to 100.

Bonds to 10 and 20 and doubles

GRAB! Bonds to 10 and doubles posters

$1 + 9 = 10$

$2 + 8 = 10$

$3 + 7 = 10$

$4 + 6 = 10$

$5 + 5 = 10$

$5 + 5 = 10$

$6 + 6 = 12$

$7 + 7 = 14$

$8 + 8 = 16$

$9 + 9 = 18$

Add the bond to 10 or double first to answer these.

1. $4 + 7 + 6 = \Box$

2. $9 + 8 + 1 = \Box$

3. $2 + 6 + 8 = \Box$

4. $7 + 9 + 3 = \Box$

5. $6 + 5 + 4 = \Box$

6. $9 + 9 + 2 = \Box$

7. $1 + 5 + 9 = \Box$

8. $5 + 6 + 6 = \Box$

9. $3 + 3 + 7 = \Box$

10. $4 + 8 + 8 = \Box$

11. $6 + 7 + 7 = \Box$

12. $6 + 8 + 4 = \Box$

13. $3 + 10 + 7 = \Box$

14. $6 + 10 + 6 = \Box$

15. $2 + 11 + 8 = \Box$

16. $11 + 5 + 5 = \Box$

I am confident with bonds to 10 and doubles.

1. 9 + 13 + 1 = ☐

2. 9 + 8 + 1 = ☐

3. 2 + 11 + 8 = ☐

4. 13 + 10 + 7 = ☐

5. 6 + 11 + 6 = ☐

6. 9 + 12 + 9 = ☐

7. 9 + 7 + 7 = ☐

8. 8 + 8 + 12 = ☐

9. 8 + 5 + 4 + 2 = ☐

10. 4 + 6 + 5 + 6 = ☐

11. 7 + 1 + 3 + 9 = ☐

12. 9 + 5 + 11 + 4 = ☐

13. 7 + 6 + 7 + 6 = ☐

14. 13 + 5 + 9 + 2 = ☐

 Choose four numbers below. Find the total. How many different answers can you make?

| 7 | 3 | 4 | 6 | 7 | 6 |

Complete these additions.

1. $8 + 3 + 8 + 7 = \boxed{}$

2. $6 + 9 + 2 + 9 = \boxed{}$

3. $7 + 7 + 6 + 8 = \boxed{}$

4. $5 + 9 + 2 + 5 = \boxed{}$

5. $4 + 4 + 9 + 2 = \boxed{}$

6. $9 + 6 + 9 + 6 = \boxed{}$

7. $8 + 6 + 6 + 2 = \boxed{}$

8. $6 + 5 + 4 + 7 = \boxed{}$

9. $8 + 9 + 6 + 1 = \boxed{}$

10. $9 + 3 + 6 + 2 = \boxed{}$

11. $8 + 3 + 12 = \boxed{}$

12. $11 + 2 + 9 = \boxed{}$

13. $14 + 14 + 1 = \boxed{}$

14. $17 + 6 + 3 = \boxed{}$

15. $7 + 11 + 11 = \boxed{}$

16. $13 + 4 + 13 = \boxed{}$

17. $14 + 6 + 5 = \boxed{}$

18. $8 + 5 + 12 = \boxed{}$

19. $12 + 6 + 12 = \boxed{}$

20. $14 + 9 + 6 = \boxed{}$

 **THINK**

Three numbers have a total of 30.
Two of the numbers are the same.
What could the numbers be?

I am confident with bonds to 10 and 20 and doubles.

9

Adding and subtracting 1-digit numbers

Use the patterns to help you answer the four questions in each set.

① 5 + 3 = ☐   35 + 3 = ☐

15 + 3 = ☐   65 + 3 = ☐

⑦ 9 − 2 = ☐   49 − 2 = ☐

19 − 2 = ☐   79 − 2 = ☐

② 3 + 6 = ☐   53 + 6 = ☐

13 + 6 = ☐   83 + 6 = ☐

⑧ 8 − 5 = ☐   58 − 5 = ☐

28 − 5 = ☐   98 − 5 = ☐

③ 2 + 7 = ☐   42 + 7 = ☐

12 + 7 = ☐   72 + 7 = ☐

⑨ 14 − 6 = ☐   44 − 6 = ☐

24 − 6 = ☐   94 − 6 = ☐

④ 8 + 5 = ☐   48 + 5 = ☐

18 + 5 = ☐   88 + 5 = ☐

⑩ 16 − 8 = ☐   56 − 8 = ☐

36 − 8 = ☐   76 − 8 = ☐

⑤ 7 + 4 = ☐   47 + 4 = ☐

17 + 4 = ☐   77 + 4 = ☐

Can you see the patterns?

⑥ 8 + 6 = ☐   38 + 6 = ☐

18 + 6 = ☐   68 + 6 = ☐

I am confident with adding and subtracting 1-digit numbers.

① 25 − 9 = ☐

65 − 9 = ☐

② 47 + 6 = ☐

77 + 6 = ☐

③ 39 + 3 = ☐

89 + 3 = ☐

④ 22 − 7 = ☐

72 − 7 = ☐

⑤ 53 + 8 = ☐

83 + 8 = ☐

⑥ 45 + 6 = ☐

85 + 6 = ☐

⑦ 28 − 9 = ☐

68 − 9 = ☐

⑧ 48 + 7 = ☐

78 + 7 = ☐

⑨ 21 − 8 = ☐

61 − 8 = ☐

⑩ 44 + 7 = ☐

74 + 7 = ☐

Now try these.

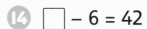

⑪ ☐ + 3 = 39

⑫ 59 − ☐ = 51

⑬ 32 + 7 = ☐

⑭ ☐ − 6 = 42

⑮ 48 + ☐ = 54

⑯ ☐ + 8 = 32

I am confident with adding and subtracting 1-digit numbers.

① 64 + 3 = ☐

② 64 + 7 = ☐

③ 48 − 5 = ☐

④ 42 − 5 = ☐

⑤ 53 + 6 = ☐

⑥ 57 + 6 = ☐

⑦ 97 − 5 = ☐

⑧ 92 − 5 = ☐

⑨ 26 + 5 = ☐

⑩ 26 + 9 = ☐

⑪ 88 − 7 = ☐

⑫ 83 − 7 = ☐

⑬ 35 + 4 = ☐

⑭ 35 + 8 = ☐

⑮ 76 − 3 = ☐

⑯ 76 − 9 = ☐

 Write different ways to make this sentence true.
Put one digit in each box.

 + =

How many different ways can you find?

I am confident with adding and subtracting 1-digit numbers.

3-digit numbers

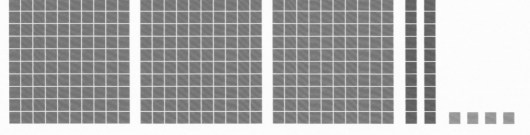

300 + 20 + 4 = 324

Copy and fill in the missing numbers.

1

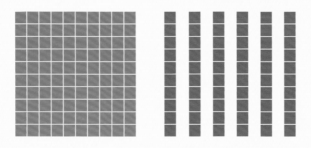

⬭ + ⬭ + ⬭ = 163

2 ⬭ + ⬭ + ⬭ = 642

3 ⬭ + ⬭ + ⬭ = 417

4 500 + 60 + 9 = ☐☐☐

5 800 + 30 + 1 = ☐☐☐

○ **I am confident with place value of 3-digit numbers.**
○
○

13

Write these numbers in figures.

	100s	10s	1s
one hundred and fifty-seven	1	5	7

1 three hundred and forty-five

2 six hundred and eighty-two

3 nine hundred and thirty-nine

4 four hundred and thirteen

5 five hundred and sixty-four

6 $\boxed{300}$ + $\boxed{60}$ + $\boxed{7}$ = ☐☐☐

7 $\boxed{600}$ + $\boxed{20}$ + $\boxed{2}$ = ☐☐☐

8 $\boxed{700}$ + ☐ + $\boxed{4}$ = $\boxed{754}$

9 ☐ + $\boxed{10}$ + $\boxed{5}$ = $\boxed{315}$

10 ☐ + $\boxed{70}$ + ☐ = $\boxed{273}$

11 ☐ + ☐ + $\boxed{1}$ = $\boxed{491}$

12 ☐ + ☐ + ☐ = $\boxed{832}$

I am confident with place value of 3-digit numbers.

364
364 – 60 = 304

472
472 – 2 = 470

1 548

5 333

2 225

6 564

3 293

7 937

4 484

8 218

Write an addition or subtraction to make all the digits in the answer the same as the purple digit.

473 + 300 + 4 = 777

628 + 200 + 60 = 888

385 – 50 – 2 = 333

9 914

13 249

10 375

14 426

11 302

15 705

12 580

I am confident with place value of 3-digit numbers.

Write each pair of numbers and use the > or < sign to show which number is greater.

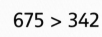 675 > 342

1 321   470

2 737   373

3 783   786

4 299   311

5 887   878

6 465   456

Write a number to make each statement true.

7 ☐ > 326

8 163 < ☐

9 ☐ < 177

10 ☐ < 586

11 306 < ☐

12 444 > ☐

13 Write a number between 423 and 456.

14 Write a number between 267 and 342.

I am confident with ordering 3-digit numbers and using greater than and less than signs.

Adding or subtracting multiples of 10 and near-multiples of 10

1	2	3	4	5	6	7	8
11	12	13	14	15	16	17	
21	22	23	24	25	26		
31	32	33	34	35			
41	42	43	44				

$24 + 19 = \square$

$24 + 19 = 43$

GRAB! A 100-square

1 17 + 20 = $\square$

2 34 – 20 = $\square$

3 35 + 30 = $\square$

4 18 + 50 = $\square$

5 49 – 20 = $\square$

6 43 + 30 = $\square$

7 56 – 40 = $\square$

8 33 + 60 = $\square$

9 21 + 70 = $\square$

10 67 – 30 = $\square$

11 18 + 80 = $\square$

12 93 – 60 = $\square$

13 25 + 70 = $\square$

14 82 – 50 = $\square$

THINK A multiple of 10 is added to a number. The total is 84. How many different possible additions are there?

○
○ **I am confident with adding and subtracting**
○ **multiples of 10 to or from 2-digit numbers.**

17

1	2	3	4	5	6	7	8
11	12	13	14	15	16	17	
21	22	23	24	25	26		
31	32	33	34	35			
41	42	43	44				

43 − ☐ = 13

43 − 30 = 13

Try these using a 100-square if it helps.

1 24 + ☐ = 44

2 35 − ☐ = 15

3 22 + ☐ = 52

4 86 − ☐ = 56

5 43 + ☐ = 93

6 21 + ☐ = 81

7 67 − ☐ = 27

8 16 + ☐ = 96

9 45 + 51 = ☐

10 83 − 21 = ☐

11 35 + 29 = ☐

12 56 − 41 = ☐

13 73 − 31 = ☐

14 28 + 69 = ☐

15 67 − 31 = ☐

16 18 + 79 = ☐

○
○ **I am confident with adding and subtracting**
○ **near-multiples of 10.**

Answer these additions.

1. 24 + 21 = ☐

2. 34 + 13 = ☐

3. 43 + 22 = ☐

4. 54 + 26 = ☐

5. 27 + 44 = ☐

6. 48 + 43 = ☐

7. 66 + 25 = ☐

8. 28 + 47 = ☐

Answer these subtractions.

9. 67 – 32 = ☐

10. 85 – 41 = ☐

11. 79 – 57 = ☐

12. 68 – 26 = ☐

13. 75 – 35 = ☐

14. 66 – 45 = ☐

15. 94 – 62 = ☐

16. 97 – 33 = ☐

17. 82 – 51 = ☐

18. 89 – 47 = ☐

19. **Choose at least four of your subtractions. Check your answers using addition.**

THINK Two numbers have a difference of 21 and a total of 85. What are the two numbers?

I am confident with adding and subtracting two 2-digit numbers.

Write these additions and complete them.

1. $48 + 36 = \boxed{}$

2. $54 + \boxed{} = 89$

3. $\boxed{} + 43 = 78$

4. $34 + 66 = \boxed{}$

5. $\boxed{} + 32 = 67$

6. $27 + \boxed{} = 89$

7. $58 + 44 = \boxed{}$

8. $\boxed{} + 35 = 98$

9. $68 + 37 = \boxed{}$

10. $16 + 85 = \boxed{}$

Write these subtractions and complete them.

11. $83 - 42 = \boxed{}$

12. $96 - 43 = \boxed{}$

13. $79 - 57 = \boxed{}$

14. $68 - \boxed{} = 24$

15. $59 - 35 = \boxed{}$

16. $77 - \boxed{} = 32$

17. $57 - \boxed{} = 23$

18. $95 - \boxed{} = 51$

19. $\boxed{} - 33 = 25$

20. $\boxed{} - 17 = 41$

21. $88 - 27 = \boxed{}$

22. $\boxed{} - 45 = 34$

 **THINK**   Two numbers have a difference of 21 and a total of 91. What are the two numbers?

I am confident with adding and subtracting two 2-digit numbers.

Write these additions and subtractions and complete them.

1. $49 + 33 = \boxed{}$

2. $86 - 63 = \boxed{}$

3. $34 + \boxed{} = 79$

4. $\boxed{} - 43 = 35$

5. $51 + \boxed{} = 97$

6. $53 + 55 = \boxed{}$

7. $79 - 46 = \boxed{}$

8. $97 - \boxed{} = 43$

9. $68 + 35 = \boxed{}$

10. $56 - \boxed{} = 24$

11. $\boxed{} + 27 = 98$

12. $64 + \boxed{} = 96$

| 1 | 2 | 3 | 4 | 5 | 6 | 7 | 8 |

THINK Arrange five of the digit cards to make this subtraction true.

 –  = q

Try doing it another way.

GRAB! A bead string

$7 \times 5 = 35$

1 $6 \times 10 = \boxed{}$

2 $9 \times 5 = \boxed{}$

3 $7 \times 10 = \boxed{}$

4 $\boxed{} \times 5 = 25$

5 $\boxed{} \times 10 = 90$

6 $6 \times 5 = \boxed{}$

7 $\boxed{} \times 10 = 60$

8 $\boxed{} \times 5 = 40$

9 $\boxed{} \times 10 = 40$

10 $50 \div 5 = \boxed{}$

11 $80 \div 10 = \boxed{}$

I am confident with multiplying and dividing by 5 and 10.

Complete these multiplications.

1 $3 \times 4 = \square$

2 $5 \times 4 = \square$

3 $7 \times 4 = \square$

4 $2 \times 4 = \square$

5 $1 \times 4 = \square$

6 $10 \times 4 = \square$

7 $9 \times 4 = \square$

8 $4 \times 4 = \square$

9 $\square \times 4 = 24$

10 $\square \times 4 = 12$

11 $\square \times 4 = 44$

12 $\square \times 4 = 48$

13 $\square \times 4 = 32$

14 $\square \times 4 = 36$

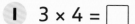

Complete these divisions.

15 $4 \div 4 = \square$

16 $8 \div 4 = \square$

17 $20 \div 4 = \square$

18 $28 \div 4 = \square$

19 $32 \div 4 = \square$

20 $48 \div 4 = \square$

Solve these problems.

21 Cows have 4 legs. How many legs on 12 cows?

22 There are 24 children. They get into groups of 4. How many groups?

 **THINK** How many multiples of 4 under 50 are also multiples of 10?

I am confident with multiplying and dividing by 4.

Complete these multiplications.

1 3 × 3 = ☐

2 2 × 3 = ☐

3 9 × 3 = ☐

4 5 × 3 = ☐

5 1 × 3 = ☐

6 10 × 3 = ☐

7 7 × 3 = ☐

8 4 × 3 = ☐

9 ☐ × 3 = 24

10 ☐ × 3 = 12

11 ☐ × 3 = 9

12 ☐ × 3 = 33

13 ☐ × 3 = 18

14 ☐ × 3 = 36

Complete these divisions.

15 15 ÷ 3 = ☐

16 18 ÷ 3 = ☐

17 21 ÷ 3 = ☐

18 27 ÷ 3 = ☐

19 24 ÷ 3 = ☐

20 36 ÷ 3 = ☐

Solve these problems.

21 Triangles have 3 sides. How many sides have 5 triangles?

22 There are 24 children. They get into groups of 3. How many groups?

 How many multiples of 3 under 40 are also multiples of 4?

I am confident with multiplying and dividing by 3.

Complete these multiplications and divisions.

1 3 × 3 = ☐

2 ☐ × 4 = 36

3 2 × 3 = ☐

4 16 ÷ 4 = ☐

5 9 × 3 = ☐

6 ☐ × 5 = 15

7 40 ÷ 4 = ☐

8 21 ÷ 3 = ☐

9 5 × 2 = ☐

10 ☐ × 3 = 24

11 24 ÷ 4 = ☐

12 12 ÷ 3 = ☐

13 28 ÷ 4 = ☐

14 33 ÷ 3 = ☐

15 1 × 3 = ☐

16 ☐ × 3 = 0

17 10 × 4 = ☐

18 110 ÷ 10 = ☐

19 7 × 4 = ☐

20 ☐ × 3 = 18

21 36 ÷ 4 = ☐

22 36 ÷ 3 = ☐

23 4 × 4 = ☐

24 ☐ × 4 = 32

25 3 ÷ 3 = ☐

26 48 ÷ 4 = ☐

27 55 ÷ 5 = ☐

28 24 ÷ 3 = ☐

Nearly there now!

29 How many rows of 4 onions can be made with 28 onions?

30 There are 27 children. They get into groups of 3. How many groups?

●
●
●
I am confident with multiplying and dividing by 3 and 4.

25

Doubling and halving odd and even numbers

GRAB! Place-value cards

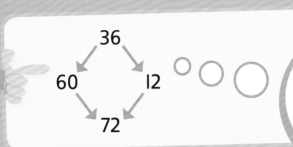

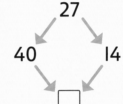

36

Double 30 is 60   Double 6 is 12

so double 36 is 72

Double each number.

1
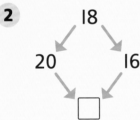

23

40   6

□

3

27

40   14

□

2

18

20   16

□

4
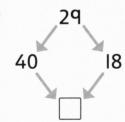

29

40   18

□

5 Double 14 is □

6 Double 16 is □

7 Double 19 is □

8 Double 17 is □

9 Double 21 is □

10 Double 24 is □

11 Double 26 is □

12 Double 28 is □

13 A number doubled is 72. What is the number?

● I am confident with doubling numbers up to 30.
○
○

Double each number.

1 12

2 18

3 23

4 24

5 16

6 29

7 17

8 26

Find the missing numbers.

9 Double 22 is ☐

10 Double 28 is ☐

11 Double 27 is ☐

12 Double ☐ is 42.

13 Double ☐ is 38.

14 Double ☐ is 52.

Solve these problems.

15 A plant was 18 cm tall. Now it is double that height. How tall is it now?

16 Before a sale, a coat cost double what it costs now. Its price now is £24. What did it cost before the sale?

17 Before a sale, a jumper cost twice what it costs now. It cost £58 before the sale. What does it cost now?

 Is this statement true or false? When a whole number is doubled the answer is always even.

● I am confident with doubles to 30.

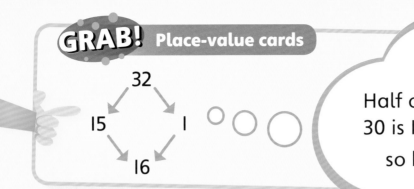

GRAB! Place-value cards

32
15 ← → 1 ○ ○ ○
↘ ↙
16

32
Half of   Half of
30 is 15   2 is 1
so half of 32 is 16

Halve each number.

1
24
10 ← → 2
↘ ↙
☐

3
22
10 ← → 1
↘ ↙
☐

2
18
5 ← → 4
↘ ↙
☐

4
38
15 ← → 4
↘ ↙
☐

5 Half of 28 is ☐

6 Half of 34 is ☐

7 Half of 26 is ☐

8 Half of 36 is ☐

9 Half of 32 is ☐

10 Half of 46 is ☐

11 A coat that cost £42 is now half price. What is its price now?

 THINK A number halved is 17. What is the number?

I am confident with halving even numbers up to 40.

Copy and complete.

Remember, $\frac{1}{2}$ is how we write half.

1 Half of 20 is ☐

Half of 4 is ☐

Half of 24 is ☐

2 Half of 20 is ☐

Half of 8 is ☐

Half of 28 is ☐

3 Half of 30 is ☐

Half of 2 is ☐

Half of 32 is ☐

4 Half of 10 is ☐

Half of 6 is ☐

Half of 16 is ☐

5 $\frac{1}{2}$ of 20 = ☐

$\frac{1}{2}$ of 6 = ☐

$\frac{1}{2}$ of 26 = ☐

6 $\frac{1}{2}$ of 30 = ☐

$\frac{1}{2}$ of 8 = ☐

$\frac{1}{2}$ of 38 = ☐

7 A DVD was £16. Now it is half-price. How much is it now?

8 There are 34 children in Class B. Half of the children are girls. How many are girls?

● **I am confident with halving numbers to 30.**

Halve each number.

1 22

2 18

3 28

4 24

5 34

6 38

7 26

8 36

Find the missing numbers.

9 Half of 16 is ☐

10 Half of 30 is ☐

11 $\frac{1}{2}$ of 25 = ☐

12 $\frac{1}{2}$ of ☐ = 12

13 $\frac{1}{2}$ of ☐ = 16

14 Half of ☐ is 13

15 $\frac{1}{2}$ of ☐ = 14

16 Half of 42 is ☐

17 $\frac{1}{2}$ of 50 = ☐

18 Half of 15 is ☐

19 In a half-price sale a DVD costs £12. How much did it cost before the sale?

20 There are 32 children in Class A. Half of the children are girls. How many are boys?

 Choose an odd number less than 20. Halve it. What do you notice? Do this several times.

● **I am confident with halves to 40.**

Find the missing numbers.

1 $14 \times 2 = \boxed{}$

2 $16 \times 2 = \boxed{}$

3 $\boxed{} \times 2 = 22$

4 $24 \times 2 = \boxed{}$

5 $\boxed{} \times 2 = 50$

6 $\boxed{} \times 2 = 28$

7 $27 \times 2 = \boxed{}$

8 $\boxed{} \times 2 = 30$

9 $29 \times 2 = \boxed{}$

10 $36 \div 2 = \boxed{}$

11 $\boxed{} \times 2 = 24$

12 $26 \div 2 = \boxed{}$

13 $32 \div 2 = \boxed{}$

14 $\boxed{} \times 2 = 34$

15 $28 \div 2 = \boxed{}$

16 $38 \div 2 = \boxed{}$

Copy and complete.

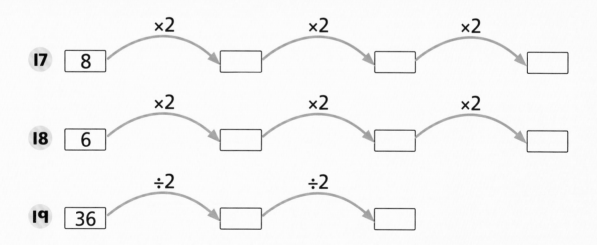

17 8 →(×2)→ ☐ →(×2)→ ☐ →(×2)→ ☐

18 6 →(×2)→ ☐ →(×2)→ ☐ →(×2)→ ☐

19 36 →(÷2)→ ☐ →(÷2)→ ☐

THINK Choose other start numbers and make two similar ×2 or ÷2 patterns of your own.

I am confident with doubling numbers to 30 and halving even numbers to 40.

January

MON	TUE	WED	THU	FRI	SAT	SUN
30	31	1	2	3	4	5
6	7	8	9	10	11	12
13	14	15	16	17	18	19
20	21	22	23	24	25	26
27	28	29	30	31	1	2

February

MON	TUE	WED	THU	FRI	SAT	SUN
27	28	29	30	31	1	2
3	4	5	6	7	8	9
10	11	12	13	14	15	16
17	18	19	20	21	22	23
24	25	26	27	28	29	1

There are 3 weeks between 3rd January and 24th January.

Work out how many weeks between each pair of dates.

1. 6th February and 20th February
2. 25th January and 1st February
3. 27th January and 24th February

Kittens leave home six weeks after their birth. What day will each kitten leave home?

4. Tabby, born 11th January
5. Tess, born 5th January
6. Mog, born 2nd January
7. Claud, born 16th January

What date is 12 days earlier than:

8. 19th January?
9. 2nd February?
10. 6th February?
11. 1st March?

12. Is the month of February shown at the top from a leap year?
13. How many days are there altogether in this year?

○ **I am confident with days and weeks of the month.**

Write the answers.

Saturday Wednesday Monday Thursday

Tuesday Sunday

Friday

1 Write the days of the week in order.

What month comes after:

2 January?

3 April?

4 October?

5 December?

What month comes before:

6 March?

7 September?

8 July?

9 January?

How many days in:

10 January?

11 3 weeks?

12 December?

13 June?

14 April and May?

15 October and November?

16 a year?

17 a leap year?

How many weeks in:

18 a year?

19 February?

20 December?

21 2 years?

THINK If the 1st January is a Tuesday how many Fridays will there be in January? What about Thursdays?

I am confident with days of the week and weeks in the year.

33

Telling the time

Write the time shown on the clock face.

quarter past 8

Write each time as it would appear on a digital clock.

5:15

I am confident with telling the time to the quarter hour on analogue and digital clocks.

Write each time as a digital time.

8:15

Write each time as an analogue time in words.
Draw the time onto a clock face.

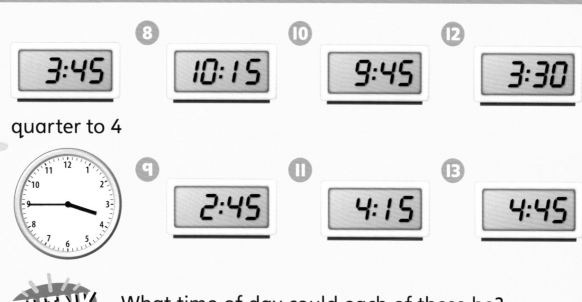

quarter to 4

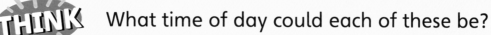

THINK What time of day could each of these be?

I am confident with telling the time to the quarter hour on analogue and digital clocks.

Write each time in words.

twenty minutes past 3

Write each time as an analogue time in words.
Draw the time onto a clock face.

6	8	10
3:50	10:20	9:25	3:35

ten minutes to 4

7	9	11
2:55	4:05	5:10

Write each in digital time.

○
○ **I am confident with telling the time to five minute**
○ **intervals on analogue and digital clocks.**

36

Write each time as a digital time.

Write each as an analogue time in words.

Write the time 10 minutes later in words.

Write the time 20 minutes later as a digital time.

I am confident with telling the time to five minute intervals on analogue and digital clocks.

3D Shape

Name each shape.

1

3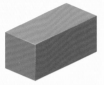

5

2

4

6

Write how many faces each shape has.

> Use 3D shapes to help you do this.

7 cube

8 cuboid

9 cone

10 cylinder

11 sphere

12 hemisphere

13 square-based pyramid

14 triangular prism

THINK Choose your favourite shape and draw it.
Write its name and two of its properties.

○
○ **I am confident with recognising and describing 3D**
○ **shapes.**

Write the 3D shapes with:

1 six faces

2 one curved face and one flat face

3 two flat faces and a curved face

4 at least one face that is a triangle

5 one curved face

6 five flat faces

7 faces that are rectangles

8 no corners (vertices)

What shape am I?

9 I can roll.
I have no edges.
I have one face.

11 I have eight vertices (corners). I have six identical faces.

10 All but one of my faces are triangles. The other face is a square.

12 I have one curved edge. One of my faces is a circle.

 Choose a 3D shape. Describe it in three ways.

I am confident with recognising and describing 3D shapes.

GRAB! A beaded number line

Write the tagged numbers.

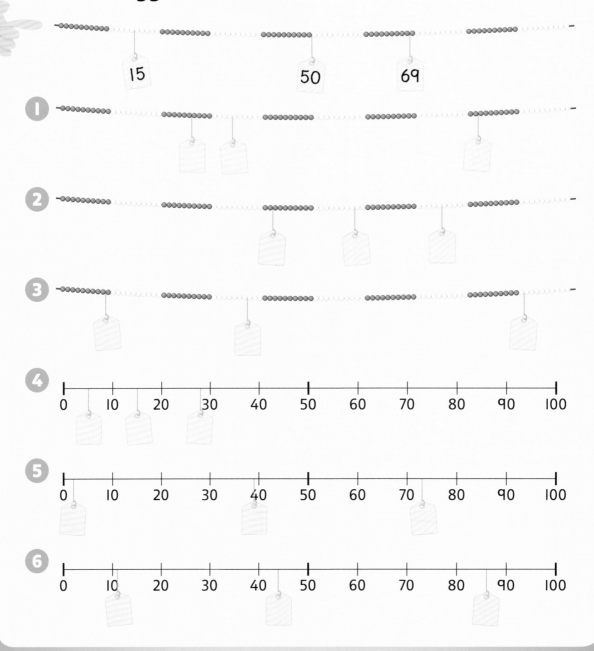

15   50   69

1

2

3

4

| 0 | 10 | 20 | 30 | 40 | 50 | 60 | 70 | 80 | 90 | 100 |

5

| 0 | 10 | 20 | 30 | 40 | 50 | 60 | 70 | 80 | 90 | 100 |

6

| 0 | 10 | 20 | 30 | 40 | 50 | 60 | 70 | 80 | 90 | 100 |

THINK Two different numbers are the same distance from the number 35. What numbers could they be? Find at least five pairs. What do you notice about them?

I am confident with placing numbers on a number line.

40

Write the tagged numbers.

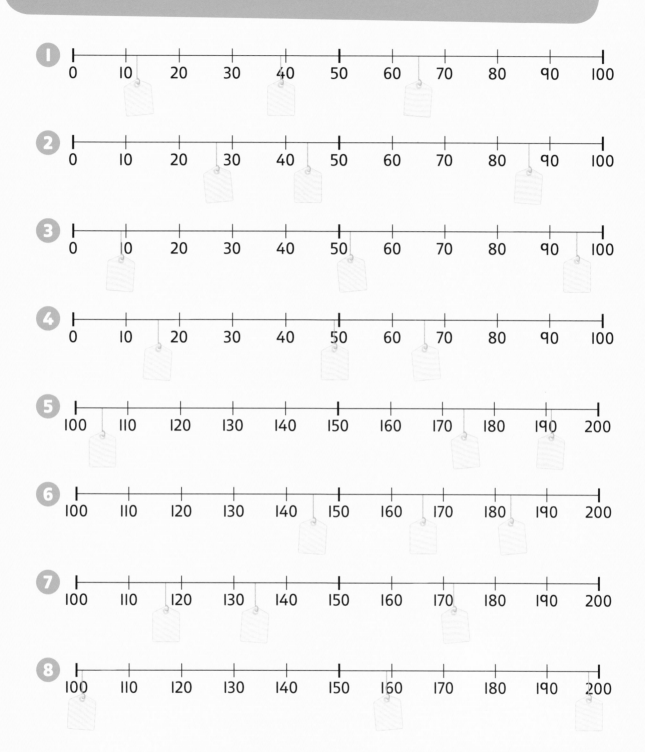

THINK Two different numbers are the same distance from the number 100. What numbers could they be? Find at least five pairs. What do you notice about them?

Draw the following number lines and mark the numbers.

① Draw a 0–100 number line and mark on 51, 26 and 80.

② Draw a 100–200 number line and mark on 127, 179 and 155.

③ Draw a 300–400 number line and mark on 384, 362 and 399.

④ Draw a 500–600 number line and mark on 551, 526 and 580.

Write each pair of numbers with a > or < sign between them.

 376 > 321

⑤ 909   990

⑥ 187   178

⑦ 488   448

⑧ 633   636

⑨ 421   419

⑩ 770   707

⑪ 842   824

⑫ 970   969

⑬ 279   297

THINK Write a number between 500 and 600 which is closer to 500. Write a number between 450 and 500 which is closer to 450. Write a number between 625 and 650 which is closer to 650.

I am confident with drawing number lines and placing numbers on, and using the greater than and less than signs.

Round the tagged number to the nearest 10.

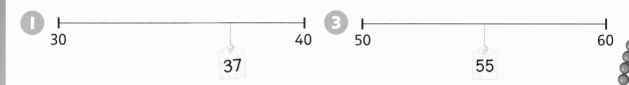

1. 30 — 40 · 37

3. 50 — 60 · 55

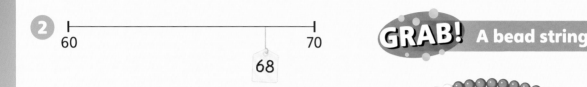

2. 60 — 70 · 68

GRAB! A bead string

Write each tagged number and round it to the nearest 10.

4. 40 — 50

6. 70 — 80

5. 80 — 90

7. 50 — 60

Do the same for each pair of lines.

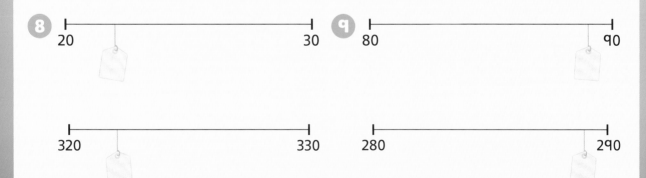

8. 20 — 30
320 — 330

9. 80 — 90
280 — 290

I am confident with rounding 2- and 3-digit numbers to the nearest 10.

Remember, if a number ends in 5 round up!

1. 43

2. 35

3. 132

4. 187

5. 437

6. 279

7. 956

8. 750

9. 525

10. 629

11. 709

12. 604

13. 396

14. 428

15. 763

16. 895

17. 206

18. 313

19. 674

20. 995

THINK Write a number which rounds to:

460	500
230	690

Copy and complete this table.

	number	round to the nearest 10	round to the nearest 100
1	389		
2	912		
3	243		
4	587		
5	298		
6	476		
7	832		
8	795		
9	509		
10	333		
11	888		
12	555		

THINK Write a rule to explain how to round to the nearest 10, and a rule to explain how to round to the nearest 100.

I am confident with rounding 3-digit numbers to the nearest 10 and 100.

$32 - 27 = 5$

Complete these subtractions.

1 $23 - 16 = \square$

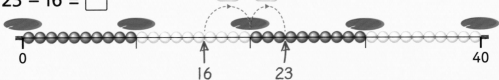

2 $34 - 28 = \square$

3 $31 - 26 = \square$

4 $53 - 47 = \square$

5 $42 - 35 = \square$

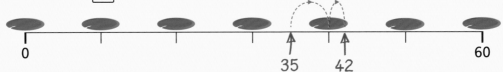

6 $54 - 46 = \square$

I am confident with subtracting by counting up.

GRAB! A number line

$48 - 34 = 14$

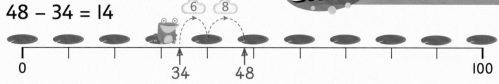

1) $164 - 156 = \boxed{}$

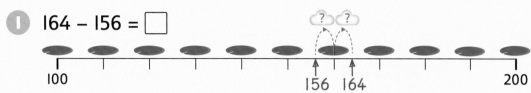

2) $223 - 215 = \boxed{}$

3) $377 - 364 = \boxed{}$

4) $486 - 478 = \boxed{}$

5) $535 - 527 = \boxed{}$

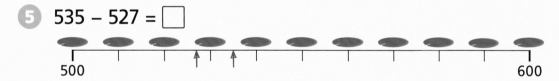

6) $649 - 636 = \boxed{}$

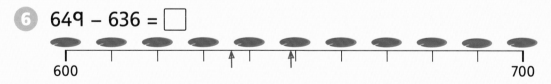

7) $768 - 753 = \boxed{}$

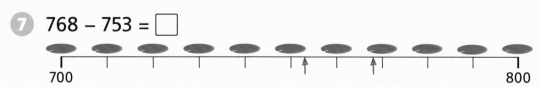

8) $854 - 849 = \boxed{}$

9) $992 - 983 = \boxed{}$

I am confident with subtracting by counting up.

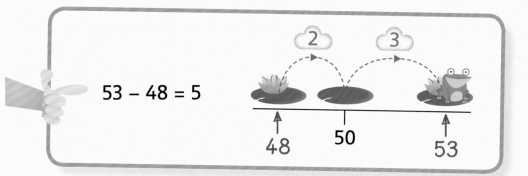

$53 - 48 = 5$

2   3

48   50   53

1. $59 - 44 = \square$
2. $64 - 57 = \square$
3. $58 - 45 = \square$
4. $43 - 31 = \square$
5. $37 - 28 = \square$
6. $63 - 51 = \square$
7. $52 - 44 = \square$
8. $74 - 62 = \square$
9. $48 - 34 = \square$
10. $83 - 75 = \square$

11. $94 - 80 = \square$
12. $80 - 67 = \square$
13. $95 - 83 = \square$
14. $73 - 62 = \square$
15. $92 - 83 = \square$
16. $85 - 77 = \square$
17. $66 - 59 = \square$
18. $71 - 65 = \square$
19. $65 - 54 = \square$
20. $83 - 69 = \square$

 Write digits to complete this subtraction:

$$3 \boxed{} - \boxed{}\boxed{} = \boxed{} 7$$

Do this several times.

I am confident with subtracting by counting up.

48

Solve these problems.

1. Jim had 52p. He bought a chocolate bar costing 44p. How much money does he have now?

2. A coat's price was £41. In a sale its price was reduced down to £33. How much money was taken off its price?

3. In July a sunflower was 86 cm tall. By August it was 94 cm tall. By how much had it grown?

4. One tiger weighs 77 kg and another weighs 85 kg. How much heavier is one than the other?

Solve these subtractions by counting back or counting up using Frog.

5. 37 − 12 = ☐

6. 63 − 21 = ☐

7. 58 − 34 = ☐

8. 93 − 51 = ☐

9. 48 − 25 = ☐

10. 94 − 63 = ☐

11. 88 − 37 = ☐

12. 66 − 24 = ☐

13. 73 − 22 = ☐

14. 93 − 31 = ☐

THINK Find at least five pairs of numbers that have a difference of 17.

I am confident with choosing the best method to perform a mental subtraction.

Double these amounts.

GRAB! Coins

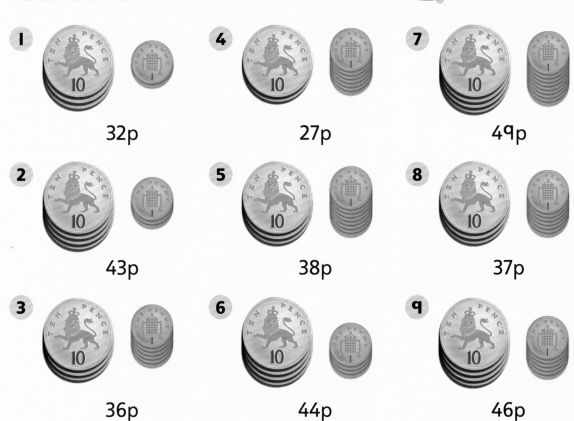

1   32p

4   27p

7   49p

2   43p

5   38p

8   37p

3   36p

6   44p

9   46p

Write the output for each number that is put into the doubling machine.

in		out	
	38		76
10	17		
11	41		
12	35		
13	22		

• I am confident with doubling up to 50.

Double each number.

1. 26

5. 48

9. 27

2. 32

6. 19

10. 38

3. 41

7. 24

11. 46

4. 37

8. 36

12. 29

Double each number.

13. 74

17. 83

21. 77

14. 82

18. 54

22. 86

15. 91

19. 58

23. 95

16. 65

20. 69

24. 78

Start with 3. Keep doubling until you are over 100.
Start with 4. Keep doubling until you are over 100.
Start with 9. Keep doubling until you are over 100.

How many odd numbers appear in your doubling sequences? Why is this?

I am confident with doubling up to and beyond 50.

Write half of each amount.

1. 82p

2. 64p

3. 86p

4. 48p

5. 62p

6. 34p

7. 70p

8. £1

9. 76p

10. 98p

11. 54p

12. 78p

Write the output for each number that is put into the halving machine.

56 → 28

13. 84

14. 74

15. 32

16. 28

in

out

Halve these numbers.

17. 7

18. 9

19. 15

20. 23

I am confident with halving even numbers up to 100 and odd numbers up to 25.

Write each input and matching output for this halving machine.

1. 66   □ (out)
2. □   38
3. 73   □
4. 95   □
5. □   29

6. What is half of 82p?

7. 33 ÷ 2 = □

8. Split 74 cm in half.

9. 49p shared between two is □

10. Halve 63.

11. Half of 55 is □

12. Divide 92 by 2.

13. 77 ÷ 2 = □

14. An 85 cm piece of ribbon is cut equally in two. How long is each piece?

15. Mr Smith gives £99 to his two sons to share equally. How much did each son get?

THINK   Find numbers less than 100 which can be halved more than twice and give a whole number as an answer. What do you notice about these numbers?

I am confident with halving odd and even 2-digit numbers.

Finding fractions of Shapes and amounts

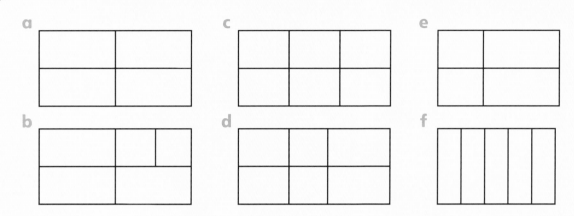

a   c   e

b   d   f

1. Which shape is divided into $\frac{1}{4}$s?

2. Which shape is divided into $\frac{1}{6}$s?

3. Which shape is divided into $\frac{1}{5}$s?

Write the fraction that is shaded for each shape.

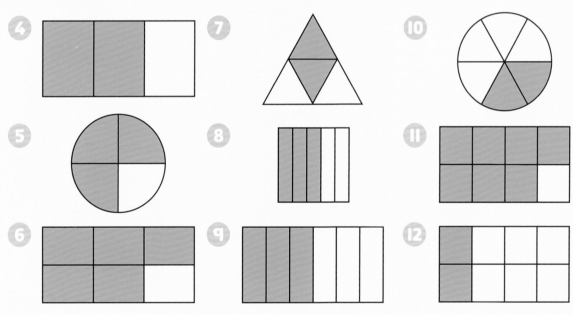

4   7   10

5   8   11

6   9   12

THINK Can you write any of the fractions above using smaller numbers?

○
○ **I am confident with recognising fractions as equal**
○ **parts of a whole.**

What fraction of each shape is shaded?

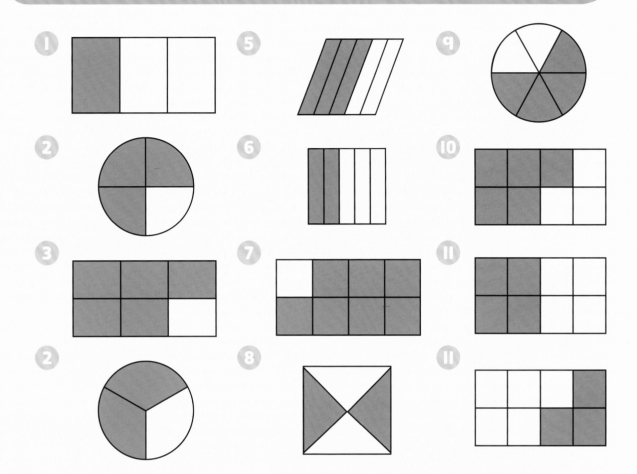

Write > or < between each pair of fractions.

13 $\frac{1}{6}$ $\frac{1}{8}$

14 $\frac{1}{4}$ $\frac{1}{3}$

15 $\frac{1}{3}$ $\frac{1}{5}$

16 $\frac{1}{6}$ $\frac{1}{5}$

17 $\frac{1}{8}$ $\frac{1}{3}$

18 $\frac{1}{6}$ $\frac{1}{4}$

Is this statement true or false?
For unit fractions (those that have the numerator 1) the larger the denominator, the smaller the fraction.

I am confident with recognising fractions as equal parts of a whole, and comparing fractions.

GRAB! Fraction strips

$\frac{1}{4}$ of 12 = 3

1   $\frac{1}{3}$ of 15 = ☐

2   $\frac{1}{2}$ of 10 = ☐

3   $\frac{1}{3}$ of 9 = ☐

4   $\frac{1}{4}$ of 16 = ☐

5   $\frac{1}{3}$ of 12 = ☐

6   $\frac{1}{4}$ of 8 = ☐ $\frac{3}{4}$ of 8 = ☐

7   $\frac{1}{3}$ of 18 = ☐ $\frac{2}{3}$ of 18 = ☐

8   $\frac{1}{4}$ of 20 = ☐ $\frac{3}{4}$ of 20 = ☐

I am confident with recognising fractions as equal parts of an amount, and finding fractions of amounts.

Find these fractions.

1. $\frac{1}{3}$ of 30 = ☐

2. $\frac{1}{2}$ of 14 = ☐

3. $\frac{1}{4}$ of 24 = ☐

4. $\frac{1}{8}$ of 16 = ☐

5. $\frac{1}{5}$ of 20 = ☐

6. $\frac{1}{4}$ of 44 = ☐

7. $\frac{1}{6}$ of 12 = ☐

8. $\frac{1}{8}$ of 80 = ☐

9. $\frac{1}{3}$ of 18 = ☐

10. $\frac{1}{5}$ of 35 = ☐

Use a fraction strip to help you.

11. Find: $\frac{1}{6}$ of 18

$\frac{5}{6}$ of 18

12. Find: $\frac{1}{5}$ of 30

$\frac{4}{5}$ of 30

13. Find: $\frac{1}{3}$ of 24

$\frac{2}{3}$ of 24

14. Find: $\frac{1}{8}$ of 80

$\frac{3}{8}$ of 80

 **THINK** Explain to a partner how you find a non-unit fraction of an amount, for example, $\frac{2}{5}$ of 20.

I am confident with finding unit and non-unit fractions of amounts.

57

Copy and complete.

Find $\frac{1}{5}$ first.

1. $\frac{2}{5}$ of 15 = ☐

2. $\frac{3}{4}$ of 16 = ☐

3. $\frac{2}{3}$ of 9 = ☐

4. $\frac{3}{8}$ of 16 = ☐

5. $\frac{4}{5}$ of 20 = ☐

6. $\frac{5}{6}$ of 12 = ☐

7. $\frac{3}{5}$ of 25 = ☐

8. $\frac{5}{6}$ of 18 = ☐

9. $\frac{5}{8}$ of 40 = ☐

10. $\frac{5}{6}$ of 30 = ☐

11. $\frac{3}{8}$ of 24 = ☐

12. $\frac{3}{5}$ of 35 = ☐

What fractions are the red counters?

13. ○○○○○○●●●●●●

14. ○○○○○○○○○○○○○○○●●●●●

15. ○○○○○○○○○○○○○○○○
    ○○○○○○○○●●●●●●

16. ○○○○○○○○●●●●●●●●●●

17. ○○○○○○○○○○○○○○○○○●●

I am confident with finding unit and non-unit fractions of amounts.

Place value of money

Find these totals.

1

2

3

4

Draw the coins you need to make these amounts.

5 £2·64

6 £3·25

7 £1·81

8 £2·53

Write the total amounts.

9 £3 + 57p = ☐

10 £2·50 + 6p = ☐

11 £1·20 + 18p = ☐

12 £1·35 + 21p = ☐

13 £3·22 + 47p = ☐

14 £2·90 + 50p = ☐

 Find at least three different ways to make £1.

● I am confident with making pounds and pence
○ amounts.
○

59

Write the missing amounts.

1. £5 + 20p + 9p = ☐

2. £2 + 10p = ☐

3. £1 + 50p + 8p = ☐

4. £2 + 42p = ☐

5. £5 + £1 + 20p = ☐

6. £3·20 + 10p = ☐

7. £1·25 + £2 + 3p = ☐

8. £6·10 + 55p = ☐

9. £2·20 + 8p = ☐

10. £3·30 + 16p = ☐

11. £1 + £3·60 + 4p = ☐

12. £6 + £1·28 = ☐

13. £6·20 + ☐ = £6·29

14. £4 + ☐ = £4·27

15. £5·25 + ☐ = £5·35

16. £1 + ☐ = £2·10

17. £3·10 + ☐ = £3·16

18. £5 + ☐ = £5·42

19. ☐ + 88p = £1·88

20. ☐ + £4 = £5·50

21. £3·14 + ☐ = £3·20

22. £2·50 + ☐ = £4·50

23. £6 + 40p + ☐ = £6·47

24. ☐ + £2·55 = £2·75

THINK I have an amount between £3 and £4. The amount can be made with four different coins. What could the amount be? Find at least ten answers.

I am confident with making pounds and pence amounts.

Find these totals.

1

2

3

4

5

Write the missing amounts.

6 £6·07 + ☐ = £6·47

7 £2·14 + £1·05 = ☐

8 £3·20 + ☐ = £4·70

9 £1·35 + £2·03 = ☐

10 £3·05 + ☐ = £3·49

11 ☐ + £3·30 = £5·75

12 £6·04 + 55p = ☐

13 ☐ + £1·01 = £3·57

14 £4·14 + £3·06 = ☐

15 £5 + ☐ = £7·09

16 ☐ + 82p = £3·99

17 ☐ + £4 = £5·42

18 £2·51 + ☐ = £4·53

19 ☐ + £1·03 = £5·95

I am confident with adding amounts of money.

61

Making 100

1. $60 + \boxed{} = 100$

2. $45 + \boxed{} = 100$

3. $75 + \boxed{} = 100$

4. $35 + \boxed{} = 100$

5. $36 + \boxed{} = 100$

6. $62 + \boxed{} = 100$

$54 + \boxed{} = 100$ ○ ◯ $\boxed{54 + 6 + 40}$ $54 + 46 = 100$

7. $73 + \boxed{} = 100$ ○ ◯ $\boxed{73 + 7 + \boxed{}}$

8. $38 + \boxed{} = 100$ ○○○○○○○○○ $\boxed{38 + 2 + \boxed{}}$

9. $47 + \boxed{} = 100$

10. $61 + \boxed{} = 100$

11. $26 + \boxed{} = 100$

12. $18 + \boxed{} = 100$

13. $53 + \boxed{} = 100$

14. $29 + \boxed{} = 100$

○○ **I am confident with all number bonds to 100.**

Complete these additions.

24 + ☐ = 100 ○ ○ (24 + 6 + 70) 24 + 76 = 100

1 41 + ☐ = 100

6 ☐ + 43 = 100

2 ☐ + 58 = 100

7 56 + ☐ = 100

3 34 + ☐ = 100

8 ☐ + 16 = 100

4 ☐ + 82 = 100

9 61 + ☐ = 100

5 77 + ☐ = 100

10 ☐ + 29 = 100

Complete these subtractions.

11 100 − 22 = ☐

16 100 − 66 = ☐

12 100 − 37 = ☐

17 100 − 7 = ☐

13 100 − 76 = ☐

18 100 − 24 = ☐

14 100 − 48 = ☐

19 100 − 57 = ☐

15 100 − 83 = ☐

20 100 − 13 = ☐

 **THINK** Using the digits 1-9 how many ways can you complete this calculation? Use each digit only once in a calculation.

 **+**  **= 100**

63

Adding and subtracting by partitioning

GRAB! Base 10 equipment and place-value cards

35 + 46

30 + 40 = 70 5 + 6 = 11

$70 + 11 = 81$

Add these by partitioning.

1 54 + 37 = ☐

2 17 + 65 = ☐

3 28 + 34 = ☐

4 48 + 36 = ☐

5 29 + 43 = ☐

6 33 + 38 = ☐

7 57 + 26 = ☐

8 68 + 27 = ☐

9 16 + 78 = ☐

10 48 + 35 = ☐

11 18 + 25 + 34 = ☐

○
○ I am confident with adding 2-digit numbers by
○ partitioning.

① 35 + 42 = ☐

② 26 + 31 = ☐

③ 64 + 25 = ☐

④ 33 + 43 = ☐

⑤ 52 + 37 = ☐

⑥ 25 + 47 = ☐

⑦ 36 + 35 = ☐

⑧ 35 + 48 = ☐

⑨ 27 + 47 = ☐

⑩ 45 + 46 = ☐

⑪ 28 + 66 = ☐

⑫ 35 + 39 = ☐

⑬ 55 + 27 = ☐

⑭ 49 + 42 = ☐

⑮ 25 + 48 = ☐

⑯ 38 + 47 = ☐

⑰ ☐ – 42 = 23

⑱ ☐ – 35 = 22

⑲ ☐ – 47 = 36

⑳ ☐ – 58 = 27

These last ones are not as hard as they look.

Check your answers to questions 17 to 20 using addition.

㉑ Jade has money in two purses. She has 26p in one and 62p in another. How much has she altogether?

㉒ Mel's dad weighs 46 kg more than Mel. Mel weighs 28 kg. How much does her dad weigh?

Write as many addition questions as you can using the digits 4, 5, 6 and 7, and answer them.

I am confident with adding 2-digit numbers by partitioning.

Perform these calculations using partitioning.

1. 25 + 49 = ☐
2. 36 + 57 = ☐
3. 64 + 18 = ☐
4. 47 + 23 = ☐
5. 56 + 43 = ☐
6. 34 + 72 = ☐
7. 63 + 45 = ☐
8. 97 + 8 = ☐
9. 12 + 89 = ☐
10. 67 + 36 = ☐
11. 82 + 24 = ☐
12. 68 + 45 = ☐

13. 48 + 56 = ☐
14. 25 + 89 = ☐
15. 55 + 57 = ☐
16. 69 + 62 = ☐
17. 75 + 48 = ☐
18. 88 + 37 = ☐
19. ☐ – 45 = 26
20. ☐ – 37 = 48
21. ☐ – 77 = 31
22. ☐ – 58 = 47
23. ☐ – 78 = 58
24. ☐ – 62 = 89

 None of the digits in this addition is a zero. What could the mystery digits be?

 ☐☐ + 3☐ = 51

I am confident with adding and subtracting 2-digit numbers by partitioning.

Find the totals using partitioning.

1 32p   16p

$\boxed{3\,2}$ + $\boxed{1\,6}$ = $\square$

$\boxed{30}$ + $\boxed{10}$ = 40 $\boxed{2}$ + $\boxed{6}$ = 8

Total = $\boxed{}$ p

2 37p   32p

$\boxed{3\,7}$ + $\boxed{3\,2}$ = $\square$

$\boxed{30}$ + $\boxed{30}$ = 60 $\boxed{7}$ + $\boxed{2}$ = 9

Total = $\boxed{}$ p

3 42p   35p

$\boxed{4\,2}$ + $\boxed{3\,5}$ = $\square$

$\boxed{40}$ + $\boxed{30}$ = $\square$ $\boxed{2}$ + $\boxed{5}$ = $\square$

Total = $\boxed{}$ p

4 23p   35p

5 41p   37p

6 42p 23p

7  35p 37p

8 32 + 53 = $\square$

9 24 + 41 + 32 = $\square$

10 41 + 33 + 22 = $\square$

11 37 + 42 + 21 = $\square$

I am confident with adding 2-digit numbers by partitioning.

1. 35 + 48 = ☐

2. 26 + 36 = ☐

3. 68 + 41 = ☐

4. 83 + 31 = ☐

5. 53 + 56 = ☐

6. 77 + 39 = ☐

7. 85 + 47 = ☐

8. 68 + 77 = ☐

9. 33 + 43 + 15 = ☐

10. 22 + 37 + 12 = ☐

11. 25 + 47 + 24 = ☐

12. 36 + 35 + 32 = ☐

13. 22 + 35 + 61 = ☐

14. 29 + 35 + 17 = ☐

15. 38 + 57 + 22 = ☐

16. 77 + 48 + 36 = ☐

17. A sunflower was 58 cm tall. It grows 27 cm taller. How tall is it now?

18. Ela buys three tops in a sale. They cost £23, £17 and £34. How much did she pay in total?

 Find three numbers with a total of 100.

I am confident with adding two or three 2-digit numbers by partitioning.

Measuring length

Write the length of each line in centimetres.

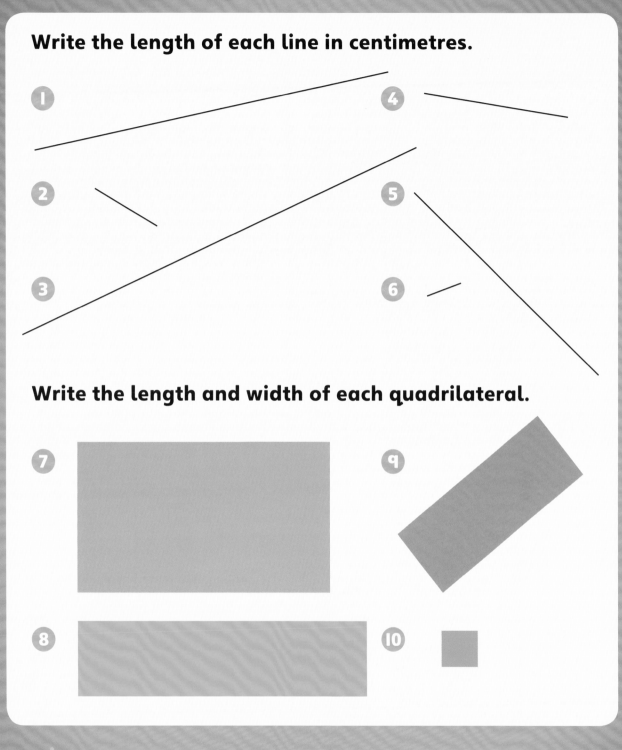

① ② ③ ④ ⑤ ⑥

Write the length and width of each quadrilateral.

⑦ ⑧ ⑨ ⑩

THINK How many centimetres of string would be needed to go all the way around the rectangle in question 7?

Write the length of each line in centimetres and millimetres.

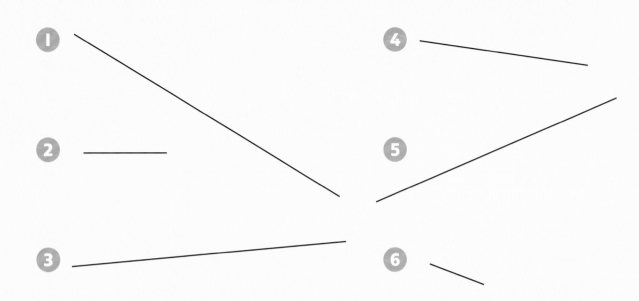

Write the lengths of all the sides of each shape in centimetres and millimetres.

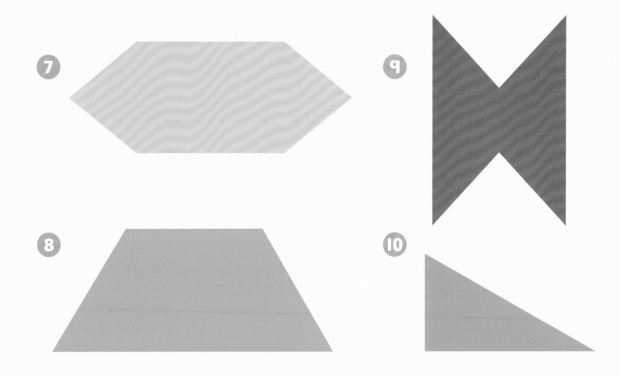

○ **I am confident with measuring to the nearest**
○ **millimetre.**
○

Draw lines of the following lengths.

1 5 cm

2 9 cm

3 12 cm

4 3 cm 4 mm

5 $6\frac{1}{2}$ cm

6 $7\frac{1}{2}$ cm

7 5 cm 8 mm

8 4 mm

9 $\frac{1}{2}$ cm

10 1 cm 9 mm

How much longer is the red worm than the blue worm in each pair?

11

12

13

14

○ I am confident with drawing and measuring lines
○ to the nearest millimetre.

71

Draw lines with these lengths:

1 5 cm 4 mm

2 7 cm 7 mm

3 2 cm 9 mm

4 8 mm

5 3·5 mm

6 10 cm 3 mm

How many millimetres in the following?

7 34 centimetres

8 18 centimetres

9 6 $\frac{1}{2}$ centimetres

10 48 centimetres

11 10 centimetres

12 2 $\frac{1}{2}$ centimetres

Write the total number of centimetres.

13 2 m 14 cm

14 6 m 62 cm

15 5 m 15 cm

16 1 m 2 cm

17 40 mm

18 120 mm

19 8 m 1 cm

20 9 m 9 cm

21 How many centimetres are there in 1000 millimetres?

22 How many metres are there in 1000 centimetres?

23 How many metres are there in 4000 millimetres?

I am confident with converting between metres, centimetres and millimetres.

Measuring capacity

How many millilitres in each jug?

50 ml

Write how many millilitres are in each.

6. 1 litre

7. $3\frac{1}{2}$ litres

8. $1\frac{1}{4}$ litres

9. $1\frac{1}{2}$ litres

10. 4 litres

11. $2\frac{1}{4}$ litres

12. $\frac{3}{4}$ litre

13. $3\frac{3}{4}$ litres

THINK   I have a 250 ml cup and a 1 litre vase. They have no measurement marks on them. What different amounts of liquid up to 3 litres can I measure with them?

 **I am confident with measuring in millilitres and converting between litres and millilitres.**

Which container holds more?

1. $\frac{1}{2}$ litre   or   400ml

2. 300ml   or $\frac{1}{4}$ litre

3. 3 litres   or   2500ml

4. 1200ml   or $1\frac{1}{4}$ litres

How much more is needed to make a litre?

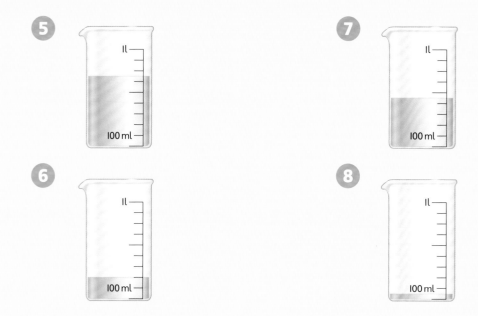

5.
6.
7.
8.

9. A carton holds 330 ml of juice. Ryan drinks 100 ml. How much is left?

10. A large mug holds $\frac{1}{2}$ litre. A small mug holds 150 millilitres less. How much does the small mug hold?

I am confident with measuring in millilitres and comparing litre and millilitre amounts.

Match each container to its most likely capacity.

1   a 30 ml

2    b 150 l

3   c 10 ml

4   d 2 l

5    e 300 ml

6    f 10 l

 How many buckets would it take to fill up a bath?

I am confident with estimating capacities.

75

Numbers on a number line

Match each tag to the correct number.

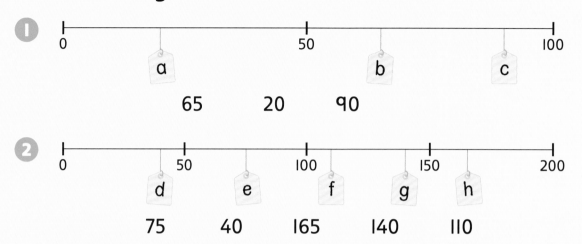

1. 65   20   90

2.

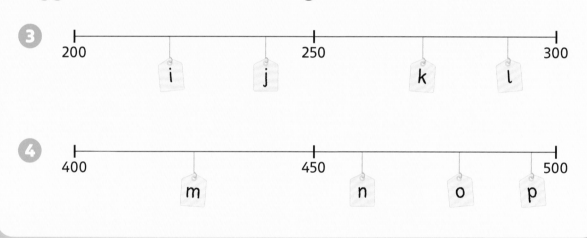

75   40   165   140   110

Suggest numbers for each tag.

3.

4.

THINK   Draw your own number line which starts at zero. Mark and label the midpoint. Mark on another point for a partner to label.

○○○ **I am confident with finding and placing numbers on a number line.**

76

Sketch the following number lines.

1 From 200 to 300. Mark 280 and circle the nearest hundred.

2 From 400 to 500. Mark 440 and circle the nearest hundred.

3 From 100 to 200. Mark 160 and circle the nearest hundred.

4 From 600 to 700. Mark 620 and circle the nearest hundred.

5 From 900 to 1000. Mark 970 and circle the nearest hundred.

Which of the numbers is the arrow pointing to?

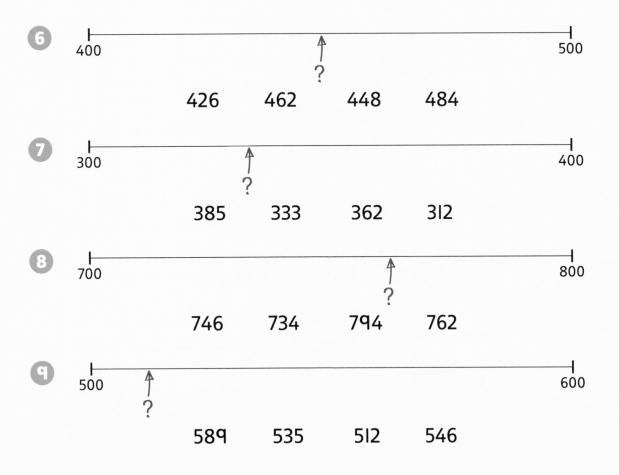

6
400 ——————————————— 500
?
426   462   448   484

7
300 ——————————————— 400
?
385   333   362   312

8
700 ——————————————— 800
?
746   734   794   762

9
500 ——————————————— 600
?
589   535   512   546

I am confident with finding and placing numbers on a number line.

77

Round these to the nearest 100.

1. 389

2. 813

3. 648

4. 761

5. 809

6. 151

7. 450

8. 960

Which of the numbers is the arrow pointing to?

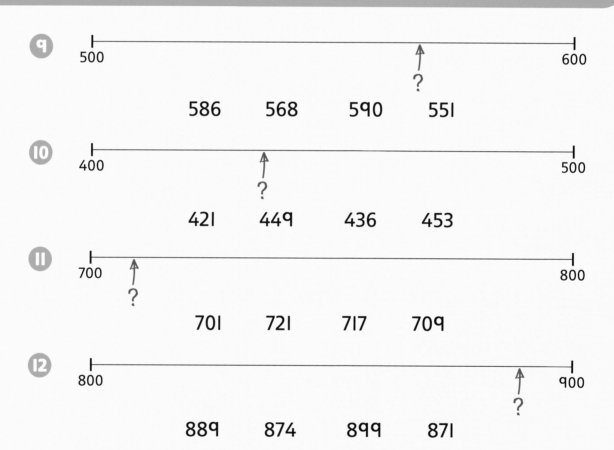

9. 500 ———————————————————↑——— 600
   ?
   586   568   590   551

10. 400 ————————↑———————— 500
    ?
    421   449   436   453

11. 700 —↑———————————————— 800
    ?
    701   721   717   709

12. 800 ———————————————————↑——— 900
    ?
    889   874   899   871

THINK Write at least ten numbers that round to 800 when rounded to the nearest 100.

I am confident with finding numbers on a number line and rounding numbers to the nearest 100.

More subtraction by counting up

1 64 – 48 = ☐

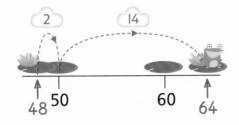

2 53 – 37 = ☐

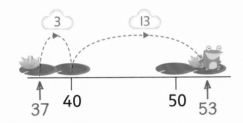

3 54 – 28 = ☐

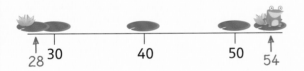

4 72 – 56 = ☐

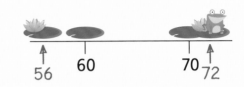

5 84 – 67 = ☐

6 92 – 66 = ☐

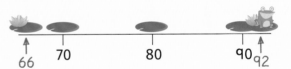

7 Before his diet, Isaak weighed 94 kg. He now weighs 77 kg. How much weight did he lose?

8 A coat costing £82 was reduced in price to £58. By how much was it reduced?

THINK Write at least five different subtraction questions with the answer 27, using 2-digit numbers.

○○○ **I am confident with subtracting by counting up to find answers between 20 and 30.**

Complete these subtractions.

1 62 – 35 = ☐

2 83 – 58 = ☐

3 74 – 46 = ☐

4 61 – 24 = ☐

5 72 – 26 = ☐

6 64 – 25 = ☐

7 85 – 37 = ☐

8 73 – 28 = ☐

9 62 – 23 = ☐

10 71 – 26 = ☐

11 84 – 45 = ☐

12 95 – 57 = ☐

13 94 – 36 = ☐

14 82 – 34 = ☐

15 86 – 27 = ☐

16 77 – 29 = ☐

17 95 – 38 = ☐

18 91 – 28 = ☐

19 81 – 35 = ☐

20 82 – 27 = ☐

21 A sunflower was 38 cm tall. It now measures 76 cm. By how much has it grown?

22 Brad had to cycle a total of 92 km. By 11 o'clock he had cycled 47 km. How much further did he have to go?

THINK Write at least five different subtraction questions with the answer 38, using 2-digit numbers.

I am confident with subtracting by counting up to find answers greater than 30.

Use the lines to work out the subtractions.

GRAB! A bead string

1 104 – 95 = ☐

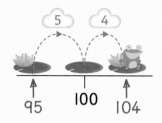

2 107 – 92 = ☐

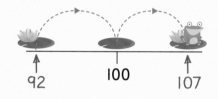

3 103 – 94 = ☐

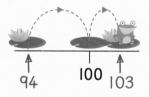

4 102 – 97 = ☐

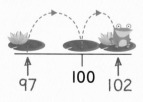

5 112 – 96 = ☐

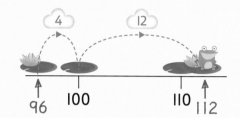

6 114 – 95 = ☐

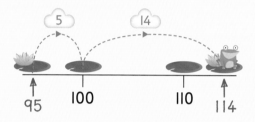

7 105 – 88 = ☐

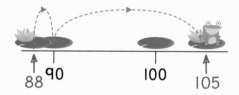

8 111 – 87 = ☐

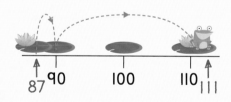

Draw number lines to work out these.

9 104 – 96 = ☐

10 112 – 98 = ☐

11 106 – 87 = ☐

12 113 – 89 = ☐

I am confident with subtracting from numbers just over 100 by counting up.

Complete these subtractions.

1. 103 – 97 = ☐

2. 102 – 94 = ☐

3. 108 – 92 = ☐

4. 107 – 93 = ☐

5. 105 – 91 = ☐

6. 109 – 94 = ☐

7. 101 – 89 = ☐

8. 103 – 87 = ☐

9. 105 – 84 = ☐

10. 111 – 98 = ☐

11. 112 – 95 = ☐

12. 116 – 93 = ☐

13. 115 – 97 = ☐

14. 113 – 88 = ☐

15. 111 – 86 = ☐

16. 115 – 87 = ☐

17. 116 – 84 = ☐

18. 117 – 78 = ☐

19. 113 – 77 = ☐

20. 115 – 79 = ☐

21. How much greater is £107 than £86?

22. How much less than 119 kg is 75 kg?

THINK Write three subtractions where Frog makes a jump of 17, having a rest on the 100 lily pad.

I am confident with subtracting from numbers over 100 by counting up, with answers up to 30.

1. Choose a number from the orange set and subtract a number from the blue set. Do this six times.

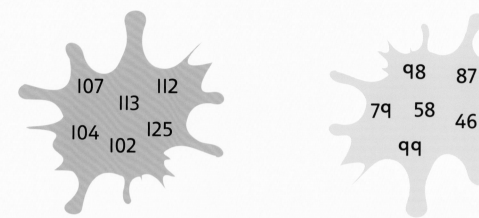

107   112
    113
104   125
    102

98   87
79   58
        46
    99

2. A spider climbed 88 cm up the wall. It then dropped to 69 cm. How far did it drop?

3. Li had 93p in change. She put 75p of it in a charity box. How much does she have now?

4. In January Paula weighed 104 kg. By December she weighs 79 kg. How much weight has she lost?

5. The distance from Bridgetown to Bury is 97 km. Jack drove 58 km before he stopped. How much further did he have to go?

6. A hamster pup weighed 48 g. Now it weighs 117 g. How much more does it weigh now?

7. A newspaper usually costs £1·14 but is reduced today to 87p. By how much has it been reduced?

I am confident with subtracting from numbers just over 100 by counting up.

83

1 **Choose two planets and find the difference.**

Is it better to use Frog or take away 10s and 1s?

113 87 63

106 95 11

Solve these word problems.

2 Mia has £78. She wants to buy a phone that costs £92. How much more money does she need?

3 I had £109. I bought a jumper for £41. How much have I got left?

4 There are 102 parents in the hall to see the school play. 76 of them are females. How many are males?

5 In the high jump Sally jumps 108 cm and Joel jumps 69 cm. How much higher does Sally jump?

THINK Write a word problem for the question 102 subtract 66 and answer it.

Revising times-tables

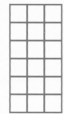 

6 × 3 = 18

3 × 6 = 18

6 × 3 = 18

3 × 6 = 18

18 ÷ 3 = 6

18 ÷ 6 = 3

Write four calculations to match each pair of arrays.

1

3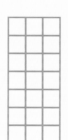

2

4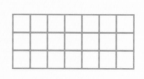

Write the two missing calculations in each set.

5 6 × 4 = 24
24 ÷ 6 = 4

7 5 × 7 = 35
7 × 5 = 35

6 27 ÷ 3 = 9
27 ÷ 9 = 3

8 4 × 7 = 28
7 × 4 = 28

THINK Draw two arrays to show the product of 8 and 4.

○
○ I am confident with writing related multiplication
○ and division facts.

85

Copy and complete the following.

1 6 × 4 = ☐   **5** 28 ÷ 4 = ☐   **9** 6 × 3 = ☐

2 3 × 5 = ☐   **6** 12 ÷ 3 = ☐   **10** 36 ÷ 4 = ☐

3 7 × 3 = ☐   **7** 45 ÷ 5 = ☐   **11** 9 × 3 = ☐

4 25 ÷ 5 = ☐   **8** 8 × 4 = ☐   **12** 33 ÷ 3 = ☐

How many 3s in each of these?

13 18   **16** 9

14 27   **17** 300

15 36   **18** 60

How many 4s in each of these?

19 16   **22** 28

20 24   **23** 48

21 32   **24** 400

How many 5s in each of these?

25 30   **28** 60

26 500   **29** 150

27 5   **30** 80

● I am confident with the 3, 4 and 5 times-tables.

Division with remainders

$$27 \div 5 = 5 \text{ r } 2$$

1 $38 \div 4 = \boxed{} \text{ r } \boxed{}$

2 $28 \div 3 = \boxed{} \text{ r } \boxed{}$

3 $34 \div 5 = \boxed{} \text{ r } \boxed{}$

4 $33 \div 10 = \boxed{} \text{ r } \boxed{}$

Each bag holds Ip coins. How many lots of 5p can you make. How many Ip coins are left over?

COINS
56p

$$56 \div 5 = 11 \text{ r } 1 \longrightarrow \text{ one Ip coin}$$

5

COINS
63p

6

COINS
21p

7

COINS
34p

8

COINS
92p

I am confident with dividing by 3, 4, 5 and 10 to find remainders.

Copy and complete these divisions.

1 $17 \div 4 = \square \, r \, \square$

2 $14 \div 3 = \square \, r \, \square$

3 $27 \div 5 = \square \, r \, \square$

4 $25 \div 10 = \square \, r \, \square$

5 $20 \div 3 = \square \, r \, \square$

6 $25 \div 4 = \square \, r \, \square$

7 $13 \div 2 = \square \, r \, \square$

8 $22 \div 3 = \square \, r \, \square$

9 $23 \div 4 = \square \, r \, \square$

10 $38 \div 5 = \square \, r \, \square$

11 $26 \div 3 = \square \, r \, \square$

12 $49 \div 10 = \square \, r \, \square$

How many triangles can be made from these matches? How many matches left over?

13 16 matches

14 20 matches

15 37 matches

16 34 matches

17 301 matches

18 11 matches

How many squares can be made from these matches? How many matches left over?

19 18 matches

20 23 matches

21 31 matches

22 38 matches

23 41 matches

24 47 matches

● I am confident with dividing by 3, 4, 5 and 10 to find
● remainders.

88

Complete these divisions.

1. $42 \div 4 = \square \, r \, \square$

2. $35 \div 3 = \square \, r \, \square$

3. $48 \div 5 = \square \, r \, \square$

4. $77 \div 10 = \square \, r \, \square$

5. $29 \div 3 = \square \, r \, \square$

6. $39 \div 4 = \square \, r \, \square$

7. $63 \div 2 = \square \, r \, \square$

8. $61 \div 3 = \square \, r \, \square$

9. $50 \div 4 = \square \, r \, \square$

10. $64 \div 5 = \square \, r \, \square$

11. $38 \div 3 = \square \, r \, \square$

12. $105 \div 10 = \square \, r \, \square$

Fill in the missing numbers.

What number divided by 4 is 10?

13. $\square \div 4 = 10$

14. $\square \div 4 = 10 \, r \, 1$

15. $\square \div 10 = 3$

16. $\square \div 10 = 3 \, r \, 1$

17. $\square \div 3 = 2 \, r \, 1$

18. $\square \div 10 = 10$

19. $\square \div 5 = 4$

20. $\square \div 5 = 4 \, r \, 1$

21. $\square \div 3 = 6$

22. $\square \div 3 = 6 \, r \, 1$

 **THINK** Write down any numbers under 100 that divide by 2, 3, 4, 5 and 10 without leaving a remainder?

I am confident with dividing by 3, 4, 5 and 10 to find remainders.

Choosing a strategy

Count on to add these.

1	2	3	4	5	6	7	8	9	10
11	12	13	14	15	16	17	18		
21	22	23	24	25	26				
31	32	33	34						
41	42								

1 $42 + 23 = \square$

2 $36 + 31 = \square$

Use partitioning to add these.

3 $36 + 48 = \square$

4 $27 + 55 = \square$ $\boxed{20}\ \boxed{7}$

Choose how best to work these out.

5 $46 + 37 = \square$

6 $53 + 19 = \square$

7 $23 + 51 = \square$

8 $58 + 26 = \square$

Count back to answer these.

9 $74 - 13 = \square$

10 $58 - 22 = \square$

Use Frog for these.

11 $65 - 38 = \square$

12 $83 - 37 = \square$

Choose how best to work these out.

13 $57 - 19 = \square$

14 $73 - 47 = \square$

15 $65 - 22 = \square$

16 $86 - 29 = \square$

17 $58 - 31 = \square$

18 $94 - 58 = \square$

THINK   Write your own additions and subtractions and choose how to work them out.

○
○   **I am confident with choosing an addition or**
○   **subtraction method.**

Choose how to work these out. You could count on or partition.

1. 46 + 31 = ☐
2. 38 + 47 = ☐
3. 53 + 58 = ☐
4. 35 + 51 = ☐
5. 48 + 39 = ☐

6. 83 + 31 = ☐
7. 77 + 38 = ☐
8. 64 + 29 = ☐
9. 56 + 76 = ☐
10. 67 + 51 = ☐

Choose how best to work these out. You could count back or use Frog to count up.

11. 85 – 19 = ☐
12. 94 – 23 = ☐
13. 83 – 28 = ☐
14. 74 – 37 = ☐
15. 95 – 51 = ☐

16. 82 – 38 = ☐
17. 77 – 29 = ☐
18. 86 – 18 = ☐
19. 64 – 26 = ☐
20. 93 – 37 = ☐

THINK Write your own additions and subtractions and choose how to work them out.

I am confident with choosing an addition or subtraction method.

<u>R</u>ead and try to imagine the story.
<u>N</u>ote the information.
Decide what <u>C</u>alculation to do.
Check it makes sense and <u>A</u>nswer the problem.

Solve these problems.

1. There are 45 cars parked on level 1 and 27 cars parked on level 2. How many cars altogether?

2. There are 63 cars parked on level 1 and 57 on level 2. How many more cars are parked on level 1 than level 2?

3. In the high jump Jo jumped 94 cm and Li jumped 78 cm. What is the difference between the heights they jumped?

4. Casper jumped 87 cm in the high jump and Chloe jumped 28 cm higher than Casper. How high did Chloe jump?

5. Mr Jones is 37 kg heavier than Mrs Jones. Mrs Jones weighs 62 kg. How heavy is Mr Jones?

6. Mr Patel is 19 kg heavier than Mrs Patel. Mr Patel weighs 84 kg. How heavy is Mrs Patel?

7. On 24th July the temperature reached 27°C during the day and fell to 14°C at night. What was the difference in temperature?

8. On 29th July the temperature was 8°C warmer than on the 28th. The temperature on the 28th was 19°C. What was the temperature on 29th?

I am confident with choosing strategies to answer addition and subtraction word problems.

<u>R</u>ead and try to imagine the story.
<u>N</u>ote the information.
Decide what <u>C</u>alculation to do.
Check it makes sense and <u>A</u>nswer the problem.

Solve these problems.

1. It takes 68 minutes from start to finish for a washing machine to wash clothes. Sam pressed 'Start' 19 minutes ago. How many minutes until it is finished?

2. A builder mixes 56 kg of sand together with 18 kg of cement and 14 kg of stones. How heavy is the mix?

3. One morning a lorry driver drove 43 km. After lunch he drove 14 km further than he had in the morning. How far did he drive altogether that day?

4. Kim has three dogs. Buster weighs 11 kg more than Jess. Jess weighs 6 kg more than Tilly. Tilly weighs 8 kg. How much does Buster weigh?

5. On 5th August the temperature in Athens, Greece was 16°C warmer than the temperature in London. The temperature in Athens was 35°C. What was the temperature in London?

6. Anna is 78 cm tall. Iska is 17 cm shorter than Anna. Cassie is 22 cm taller than Iska. How tall is Cassie?

7. Ajit is 13 cm taller than Fred and Fred is 16 cm shorter than Zack. Ajit is 93 cm tall. How tall is Zack?

I am confident with choosing strategies to answer addition and subtraction word problems.

cube puzzles

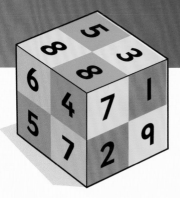

① Choose a pair of 2-digit numbers from the cube and find their total and their difference.

You can use any method you think best. For example:

29 + 88	88 – 29
20 + 80 = 100	88 – 30 = 58
9 + 8 = _17_	58 + 1 = 59
117	

29 and 88: total 117, difference 59

Can you find a pair of numbers from the cube that has:

② the total 100 and the difference 42?

③ the total 110 and the difference 4?

④ the total 93 and the difference 35?

⑤ Choose three 2-digit numbers from the cube and find the total.

⑥ Can you find three 2-digit numbers from the cube that have a total that is a multiple of 10?

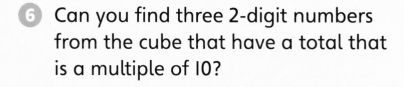

Grid puzzles

Four numbers are written in a square. Four products can be found, multiplying across and diagonally.

5	7
4	8

$4 \times 7 = 28$

$5 \times 7 = 35$

$4 \times 8 = 32$

$5 \times 8 = 40$

1 Choose four different numbers to write in a square. Find the products. Do this several times.

Can you find four numbers that give these products:

2 50, 40, 10 and 8?

3 20, 12, 35 and 21?

4 75, 85, 30 and 34?

Find the four products for each of these.

5

12	3
10	4

6

3	5
9	4

7

11	4
7	3

Series Editor
Ruth Merttens

Author Team
Jennie Kerwin and Hilda Merttens

Published by Pearson Education Limited, Edinburgh Gate, Harlow, Essex, CM20 2JE.

www.pearsonschools.co.uk

Text © Pearson Education Limited 2013
Typeset by Debbie Oatley @ room9design
Original illustrations © Pearson Education Limited 2013
Illustrated by Matt Buckley, Marek Jagucki, Debbie Oatley, Anthony Rule
Cover design by Pearson Education Limited
Cover photo/illustration by Volker Beisler © Pearson Education Limited

First published 2013

16 15 14
10 9 8 7 6 5 4 3 2

British Library Cataloguing in Publication Data
A catalogue record for this book is available from the British Library

ISBN 978 1 408 27847 5

Printed in the UK by Butler Tanner and Dennis Ltd

Acknowledgements
We would like to thank the staff and pupils at North Kidlington Primary School, Haydon Wick Primary School, Swindon, St Mary's Catholic Primary School, Bodmin, St Andrew's C of E Primary & Nursery School, Sutton-in-Ashfield, Saint James' C of E Primary School, Southampton and Harborne Primary School, Birmingham, for their invaluable help in the development and trialling of this book.

Every effort has been made to contact copyright holders of material reproduced in this book. Any omissions will be rectified in subsequent printings if notice is given to the publishers.